120 of the best quotes of Dwight Shrute

Dwight Shrute – Paper salesman, beet farmer, black belt and all round inspiration.

In this book you will find 120 of his best, most insightful quotes.

Enjoy reading them!

1

"I don't have a lot of experience with vampires, but I have hunted werewolves. I shot one once, but by the time I got to it, it had turned back into my neighbour's dog."

2

"You better learn your rules. If you don't, you'll be eaten in your sleep."

3

"Nothing stresses me out. Except having to seek the approval of my inferiors."

4

"Michael is like Mozart, and I'm like Butch Cassidy. You mess with Mozart and you're gonna get a bullet in your head, courtesy of Butch Cassidy."

5

"My perfect Valentine's day? I'm at home, three cell phones in front of me, fielding desperate calls from people who want to buy one of the fifty restaurant reservations I made over six months ago."

"I'm gonna intimidate him, OK? Watch this... So anyways, she said that is the biggest penis I have ever seen, and I said I know! That's why I brought you to the penis museum, where tickets are a thousand dollars."

7

"Everyone, follow me to the shelter. We've got enough food for 14 days. After that, we have a difficult conversation."

8

"I always wondered how they picked the person to die. I'd be good at picking the person."

9

"When my mother was pregnant with me, they did an ultrasound and found she was having twins. When they did another ultrasound a few weeks later, they discovered that I had adsorbed the other foetus. Do I regret this? No, I believe his tissue has made me stronger. I now have the strength of a grown man and a little baby."

"And I will travel to New Zealand. And walk The Lord of the Rings trail to Mordor."

11

"When I die, I want to be frozen. And if they have to freeze me in pieces, so be it. I will wake up stronger than ever, because I will have used that time to figure out exactly why I died. And what moves I could have used to defend myself better now that I know what hold he had me in."

12

"In an ideal world, I would have all 10 fingers on my left hand so my right hand could just be a fist for punching."

13

"I am better than you have ever been or ever will be."

14

"I am faster than 80 percent of all snakes."

15

"Always the Padawan, never the Jedi."

16

"There are three things you never turn your back on: bears, men you have wronged, and a dominant male turkey during mating season."

17

"All you need is love? False. The four basic human necessities are air, water, food, and shelter."

18

"I am ready to face any challenge that might be foolish enough to face me."

19

"You couldn't handle my
undivided attention."

20

"You think you're excited? You should feel my nipples. Boing!"

21

"And I misspelled, in front of the entire school, the word 'failure.'"

22

"I am fast. To give you a reference point, I am somewhere between a snake and a mongoose… and a panther."

23

"Through concentration, I can raise and lower my cholesterol at will."

24

"I really like Andy these days. He's pretended, and he does exactly as I tell him to. All that will change when real Andy comes back tomorrow. Unless he comes back as pretend Dwight. In which case, we're in for an epic, confusing showdown."

25

"I grew up on a farm. I have seen animals having sex in every position imaginable. Goat on chicken. Chicken on goat. Couple of chickens doing a goat, couple of pigs watching."

26

"Those who can't farm, farm celery."

27

"I saw Wedding Crashers accidentally. I bought a ticket for Grizzly Man and went into the wrong theatre. After an hour, I figured I was in the wrong theatre, but I kept waiting. 'Cause that's the thing about bear attacks... they come when you least expect it."

"They say that no man is an island. False! I am an island and this island is volcanic. And it is about to erupt. With the molten hot lava of strategy!"

29

"A real man swallows his vomit when a lady is present."

30

"And I did not become a Lackawanna County volunteer sheriff's deputy to make friends. And by the way, I haven't."

31

"In the wild, there is no healthcare. Healthcare is oh, I broke my leg! A lion comes and eats you, you're dead. Well, I'm not dead, I'm the lion. You're dead!"

"Congratulations on your one cousin. I have seventy, each one better than the last!"

33

"The hand that reaches from the grave to grip your throat is the strong hand you want on the wheel."

34

"Women are like wolves. If you want one, you must trap it. Snare it. Tame it. Feed it."

35

"Identity theft is not a joke, Jim!
Millions of families suffer every year."

"There are a huge number of yeast infections in this county. Probably because we're downriver from that old bread factory."

37

"I signed up for second life about a year ago. Back then, my life was so great that I literally wanted a second one. Absolutely everything was the same... except I could fly."

38

"Of course, martial arts training is relevant… Uh, I know about a billion Asians that would beg to differ… You know what, you can go to hell, and I will see you there. Burning!"

39

"The eyes are the groin of the head."

"D.W.I.G.H.T. Determined. Worker. Intense. Good worker. Hard worker. Terrific."

"Security in this office park is a joke. Last year I came to work with my spud-gun in a duffel bag. I sat at my desk all day with a rifle that shoots potatoes at 60 pounds per square inch. Can you imagine if I was deranged?"

"I come from a long line of fighters. My maternal grandfather was the toughest guy I ever knew. World War II veteran killed twenty men and spent the rest of the war in an allied prison camp. My father battled blood pressure and obesity all his life. Different kind of fight."

"No, don't call me a hero. Do you know who the real heroes are? The guys who wake up every morning and go into their normal jobs and get a distress call from the Commissioner and take off their glasses and change into capes and fly around fighting crime. Those are the real heroes."

44

"As a volunteer Sheriff's Deputy, I've been doing surveillance for years. One time I suspected an ex-girlfriend of mine of cheating on me, so I tailed her for six nights straight. Turns out... she was. With a couple of guys actually, so... mystery solved."

45

"To avoid illness, expose yourself to germs, enabling your immune system to develop antibodies. I don't know why everyone doesn't do this. Maybe they have something against living forever."

"As a farmer, I know that when an animal is sick, sometimes the right thing to do is put it out of its misery. With the electricity we are using to keep Meredith alive, we could power a small fan for two days. You tell me what's unethical."

"Dolphins get a lot of good publicity for the drowning swimmers they push back to shore, but what you don't hear about is the many people they push farther out to sea! Dolphins aren't smart. They just like pushing things."

"Once I'm officially Regional Manager, my first order of business will be to demote Jim Halpert. So, I will need a new number two. My ideal choice? Jack Bauer. But he is unavailable. Fictional. And overqualified."

49

"Reject a woman and she will never let it go. One of the many defects of their kind. Also, weak arms."

"Now that I own the building, I'm looking for new sources of revenue. And a daycare center? Muahahahahahahaha. Well, I guess it's not an evil idea, it's just a regular idea, but there's no good laugh for a regular idea."

51

"Why tip someone for a job I'm capable of doing myself? I can deliver food. I can drive a taxi. I can, and do, cut my own hair. I did, however, tip my urologist, because I am unable to pulverize my own kidney stones."

52

"Fortunately, my feelings regenerate at twice the speed of a normal man's."

53

"It's never the person who you most suspect. It's also never the person you least suspect, since anyone with half a brain would suspect them the most. Therefore, I know the killer to be Phyllis. The person who I most medium suspect."

"It's a real shame because studies have shown that more information gets passed through water cooler gossip than through official memos. Which puts me at a disadvantage because I bring my own water to work."

55

"'R' is among the most menacing of sounds. That's why they call it 'murder' and not 'mukduk.'"

"At first, I drove myself crazy thinking about the things I should have done differently. I never should have played that joke on Erin. I never should have hollowed out this damn pumpkin in the first place. Then I realized that I was being silly. I mean, the pumpkin should rot off of my head in a month or two. Right?"

57

"Yes, I have a wig for every single person in the office. You never know when you're gonna need to bear a passing resemblance to someone."

58

"OK, see you later, Pan."

59

"Jim couldn't land me in a thousand years."

"I wonder if king-sized sheets are called presidential-sized in England."

61

"I really should have a Tweeter account."

62

"Ah, humor. I have it, too."

63

"I hope the war goes on forever and Ryan gets drafted. I'm sorry, only part of me meant that. He'd probably end up a hero there, anyway."

64

"Get a friend, loser."

65

"I don't care what Jim says. This is NOT the real Ben Franklin. I am 99.9 percent sure."

66

"What is my perfect crime? I break into Tiffany's at midnight. Do I go for the vault? No, I go for the chandelier. It's priceless. As I'm taking it down, a woman catches me. She tells me to stop. It's her father's business. She's Tiffany. I say no. We make love all night. In the morning, the cops come, and I escape in one of their uniforms. I tell her to meet me in Mexico, but I go to Canada. I don't trust her. Besides, I like the cold. Thirty years later, I get a postcard. I have a son, and he's the chief of police. This is where the story gets interesting. I tell Tiffany to meet me in Paris by the Trocadero. She's been waiting for me all these years. She's never taken another lover. I don't care. I don't show up. I go to Berlin. That's where I stashed the chandelier."

"Yes, I have acted before. I was in a production of Oklahoma! In the seventh grade. I played the part of Mutey the Mailman. They had too many kids, so they made up roles like that. I was good."

"Listen up, Flenderson, you're being weak and ineffectual. I'm cowboying this meeting, OK! Here are the new rules, OK? Earth tones only. Also, women are forbidden to wear pants."

"When held over heat, the invisible ink will reveal that everyone should meet at the warehouse immediately. Do not ask me where I got the invisible ink. Urine. It was urine."

"Yes, I am taking Andy hunting after work. Not long ago we were sexual competitors. I used to hate him, hate him, hate him, hate him. I studied him, to figure out why I hated him so much. But that blossomed into a very real friendship, as these things often do."

71

"Oh, you know that line on the top of the shrimp? That's faeces."

"There was a terrible war, ugh, so many died. Far too many died. But if Frodo hadn't destroyed the ring, then goodness itself might have died."

"Michael always says, 'K-I-S-S: keep it simple, stupid.' Great advice. Hurts my feelings every time."

74

"Five minutes ahead of schedule... right on schedule."

75

"Can't a guy just buy some bagels for his friends so they'll owe him a favor which he can use to get someone fired who stole a co-manager position from him anymore? Jeez. When did everyone get so cynical?"

76

"You know, I really would've appreciated a heads up that you were into dating mothers. I would've introduced you to mine."

"Schrute Farms is very easy to find. It's right in the middle of the root vegetable district. If the soil starts to get acidic, you've gone too far."

78

"All that singing got in the way of some perfectly good murders."

"I always knew I would be destroyed by my own creation, but honestly, I thought it would be that bull that Mose and I are trying to reanimate."

Michael Scott: "Why do you have a diary?"

Dwight: "To keep secrets from my computer."

"Do I have a date for Valentine's Day? Yes. February 14th."

82

"Today, smoking is going to save lives."

83

"If I were buying my coffin, I would get one with thicker walls so you couldn't hear the other dead people."

"Schrutes don't celebrate birthdays, idiot. It started as a depression-era practicality and then, moved on to an awesome tradition that I look forward to every year!"

85

"It's not effeminate. It's festive."

"I sat at my desk all day with a rifle that shoots potatoes at 60 pounds per square inch. Can you imagine if I was deranged?"

"I studied him, to figure out why I hated him so much. But that blossomed into a very real friendship, as these things often do."

"In an ideal world, I would have all 10 fingers on my left hand so my right hand could just be a fist for punching."

"Welcome to the Hotel Hell. Check-in time is now. Check-out time is never."

"Bears are more afraid of you than you are of them? You obviously aren't scared enough."

"Love is all you need? False, you need water and rations."

"OK. When the baby emerges, mark it secretly in a kind of a mark that only you could recognize and no baby snatcher could ever copy."

"Babies are one of my many areas of expertise. Growing up, I performed my own circumcision."

"Twelve hundred dollars is what I spent on my whole bomb shelter. For that kind of money, this stroller, should be indestructible."

95

"Hold me! Cradle my hand!"

"I'm screaming! I'm screaming! I'm screaming! Aah! Numb me up! I want anesthesia!"

"Sasquatches are the strongest animal on the planet, so fine call me a Sasquatch!"

"A hero kills people, people that wish him harm. A hero is part human and part supernatural. A hero is born out of a childhood trauma, or out of a disaster, that must be avenged."

"Will I get over it? Mmm. No. But life goes on."

100

"Jim is my enemy. But it turns out that Jim is also his own worst enemy. And the enemy of my enemy is my friend. So, Jim is actually my friend. But because he is his own worst enemy, the enemy of my friend is my enemy so, actually, Jim is my enemy."

"You only live once? False. You live every day. You only die once."

"He's gone. I miss him so much. Oh, I cry myself to sleep, Jim. False. I do not miss him."

"The dictionary defines superlative as: of the highest kind, quality, or order, surpassing all else, or others; supreme. That's great. If I wanted the dictionary definition, I'd buy a dictionary. I define it as Dwight Schrute. As a sales executive, as a leader, as a man, and as a friend, he is of the highest kind, quality, and order; supreme."

"That's cool. Hey, you know what's even cooler than triceratops? Every other dinosaur that ever existed."

"You're a perfectly fine toilet. I'm just an extraordinary piece of crap."

"Before I do anything I ask myself, 'Would an idiot do that?' And if the answer is yes, I do not do that thing."

107

"Who is Justice Beaver?"

"It's a real shame because studies have shown that more information gets passed through water cooler gossip than through official memos. Which puts me at a disadvantage because I bring my own water to work."

"Jim told me you could buy gaydar online."

110

"I never thought I'd say this, but I think I ate too much bone marrow."

"PowerPoints are the peacocks of the business world; all show, no meat."

"Would I ever leave this company? Look, I'm all about loyalty. In fact, I feel like part of what I'm being paid for here is my loyalty. But if there were somewhere else that valued loyalty more highly… I'm going wherever they value loyalty the most."

"I love catching people in the act.
That's why I always whip open doors."

114

"The Civil War history industry has conveniently forgotten about the battle of Schrute Farms. Whatever. I'm over it. It's just grossly irresponsible."

"Bread is the paper of the food industry. You write your sandwich on it."

116

"It's better to be hurt by someone you know accidentally, than by a stranger on purpose."

Pam: "Dwight, am I hot right now?"

Dwight: "Why would I or anyone else think that you're hot right now? I can't impregnate you, and that's the driving force between male-female attraction."

Oscar: "Don't you want to see the baby?"

Dwight: "Psh! Why? I know what Angela and the senator look like. I can mash that up in my head right now."

"In the end, the greatest snowball isn't a snowball at all. It's fear. Merry Christmas."

"How would I describe myself? Three words: hardworking, alpha male, jackhammer, merciless, insatiable."

"I wish I could menstruate. If I could menstruate, I wouldn't have to deal with idiotic calendars anymore. I'd just be able to count down from my previous cycle. Plus, I'd be more in tune with the moon and the tides."

"People underestimate the power of nostalgia. Nostalgia is truly one of the greatest human weaknesses, second only to the neck."

"Why are all these people here?
There's too many people on this earth.
We need a new plague."

124

"When someone smiles at me, all I see is a chimpanzee begging for its life."

"Yes. I have decided to shun Andy Bernard for the next three years. Which I'm looking forward to. It's an Amish technique. It's like slapping someone with silence."

Printed in Great Britain
by Amazon